CW00327924

YORKSHIRE CURIOSITIES

compiled by
Paul Jackson

Dalesman

First published in Great Britain 2013 by Dalesman Publishing
an imprint of
Country Publications Ltd
The Water Mill, Broughton Hall
Skipton, North Yorkshire BD23 3AG

Text © Paul Jackson 2013
Illustrations © Pete Clarke 2013

ISBN 978-1-85568-317-4

Printed in China by 1010 Printing Ltd.

Introduction

With around four million acres, five million inhabitants and a history stretching back a millennium and more, Yorkshire has amassed an unbeatable collection of curiosities. The biggest and smallest, the longest and shortest — and the downright weirdest … you'll find them all within the borders of the Broad Acres.

During my time as editor of the famous *Dalesman* magazine I travelled throughout the Ridings to witness the beautiful and the bizarre of Yorkshire's diverse landscape; I listened to humorous and honest inhabitants; and I learnt of a proud and eventful history.

On the following pages I share some of the facts, oddities and myths I discovered on my journey.

Paul Jackson

Just a giant yob

Legendary giant Rombald was something of a countryside yob. Apparently, while running away from his wife, he left his huge footprint on Ilkley Moor on the rock known as the Cow, and kicked over the boulder we call the Calf.

A giant pain

Wade was another giant with little respect for the countryside. He is said to have scooped up a great handful of the North York Moors to create the Hole of Horcum before chucking it a few miles to produce Blakey Topping.

A sailor's life for me

Did you know that if you board a ship at Goole — Britain's furthest inland port — you will have to travel fifty miles (80 km) before you reach the North Sea?

Folk cure for freckles
East Riding inhabitants used to think
that dabbing freckles with blood from
a white hen would make them
vanish. Unfortunately it was more
likely to make the white hens
disappear.

How to make warts disappear

An old Yorkshire remedy for making warts disappear was to stroke them with a snail which would then be impaled on a thorn. The unfortunate snails were obviously too slow to escape when they saw a warty person heading their way.

Not quite last orders

The Bingley Arms at Bardsey, between Leeds and Wetherby, is thought to be England's oldest pub. They've been selling ale on the site for over a thousand years (wonder what the cost of a pint was in 1013?).

Dance crazy

Long-sword dancing has been
recorded in Yorkshire since 1789 and
teams such as Goathland's Plough
Stots have been around for more
than 150 years. And they said the
craze wouldn't last.

Let's skip work
In the nineteenth century
Scarborough had its own public
holiday on Shrove Tuesday when
servants and apprentices were given
half a day off. They played games
along the seafront, and today this is
marked by a skipping festival.

Standing tall

William Bradley (1787-1820) lived
with his head in the clouds — well,
almost. He was seven feet nine inches
(2.35 m) tall and weighed twenty-
seven stone (171 kg). He came from
Market Weighton and was presented
with a gold chain by George IV for
being the tallest man in Britain.

We're not mean, just careful
A chap born at Topcliffe near Thirsk
was nicknamed Old John Mealy Face
as he used to press his face into his
flour before leaving home and check
it when he returned.

Taking pride of place

Four eight-foot (2.4 m) stone lions sculpted by Thomas Milner for Trafalgar Square were rejected as being too small, so they were brought up north to take 'pride' of place in Saltaire.

Under starter's orders
Dating back to 1519, North
Yorkshire's Kiplingcotes Derby is
England's oldest flat race for horses.
I bet it is held on the third Thursday
in March.

Weight watchers

While many of us are stuffing our faces with chocolate on Easter Monday, there are some who prefer lugging a hundredweight (50 kg) of coal on their backs over a mile (1.5 km) through the West Riding town of Gawthorpe in the World Coal Carrying Championships — which started out as a bet in a pub, of course.

Wuff justice

'He's as lazy as Ludlam's dog' is an old saying from the Barnsley area. Who Ludlam was we don't rightly know, but his dog was said to be so idle that "it leeaned its 'eead agen t' wall ter bark".

Better the Devil you know
The bells of Dewsbury Parish Church have been tolled every Christmas Eve since the thirteenth century — once for every Christian year — to remind the Devil of his defeat when Jesus was born. (And 2,013 tolls can leave long-term ringing in your ears.)

Ghostly goings-on

Jenny Gallow committed suicide in a hollow near Flamborough. Folklore has it that anyone who runs round the hollow nine times will hear the girl's ghostly cry:

'Ah'll put on mi bonnet
An' tee on mi shoe,
An' if thoo's not off
Ah'll be efter thoo!"

Carved with pride
Yorkshire's White Horse was carved out of the hill above Kilburn, North Yorkshire, in 1857. The idea was conceived by Thomas Taylor, and made by local schoolmaster John Hodgson and thirty villagers.

Doe, a deer

The White Doe of Rylstone inspired
Wordsworth to write 2,000 lines of
poetry on how Francis Norton was
murdered and buried at Bolton
Priory. Norton's sister visited the
grave with her pet doe every Sunday
— and the doe continued the
pilgrimage even after the sister died.

Going, going, gone

In 1806 George Gowthorpe sold his wife for 20 guineas in Hull market place. He delivered her to a chap called Houseman with a halter around her neck. One Pontefract husband held several auctions in 1815 in a bid to sell his wife. The dear lady was eventually sold for 11 shillings. And in 1862 a Selby man succeeded in selling his missus on the steps of the market cross for a pint of ale. I hope she wasn't bitter.

Going back to the wild

"I rode over the mountains to Huddersfield. A wilder people I never saw in England…" wrote John Wesley in his diary. Must have been pay day at the mill.

Barnsley, tha knaws

Wesley also said of Barnsley:

"A place famous for all
manner of wickedness."

Must have been pay day
at the mine.

Spurned in love

When a local barmaid rejected the advances of William Sharp of Laycock near Keighley, he went home to bed and stayed there till he died (of cramp) forty-nine years later.

Anything for a quiet life

Some say that the original Darby and Joan were an old couple who lived in Healaugh, near York, who were buried together in the village churchyard.

The preacher's breeches
In 1820, at a time when breeches
were universally worn and trousers
considered vulgar, officials at the
Bethel Chapel, Cambridge Street,
Sheffield, decreed:
"Under no circumstances whatever
shall any preacher be allowed to
occupy the pulpit who wears
trousers."

Mind your head, your majesty

When King Charles I was being taken for trial in London he was knocked off his horse by a tree branch at Burn Bridge, near Harrogate. The landowner was mortified and chopped down the offending tree. Perhaps he'd have been better suggesting specs for the king.

Don't be such a boar

In 1355 Edward III, while hunting in the Forest of Knaresborough, was saved from being attacked by a wild boar thanks to the action of one Thomas Ingilby. The grateful king knighted the fearless Thomas and granted a charter to the village of Ripley.

Time for a whip-round

Obviously stuck for something to do on 18th October (St Luke's Day) the good citizens of York used to go round the alleyways whipping stray dogs. This could be the reason behind the strangely named street of Whip-ma-whop-ma-gate.

An owl-beard by any other name
Ugglebarnby (near Whitby) is one of
many strange Yorkshire place-names.
It stems from an Old Norse
nickname 'uglubarthi' meaning
owl-beard, and 'by' meaning farm.
Now all we want to know is what an
owl-beard looks like.

The water-course of true love

At Kirkby Malham Church in Malhamdale is a grave with a watercourse running down the centre. It is said to be for a sea captain and his wife, the latter insisting on this spot because water had kept them apart during his life. When the time came to bury her, the gravediggers found solid rock on her part of the grave, so she ended up in the same side as hubby.

What a carve-up

A turkey carved from wood provides support for the lectern at Boynton Church in East Yorkshire. It represents the coat of arms granted to William Strickland who first brought turkeys to Britain in the sixteenth century. Now turkeys are carved every Christmas.

Journey to the World's End
You can visit the Walls of Jericho, Jerusalem, Egypt, Moscow and World's End within a few minutes — without the aid of the internet. They're all places within a three-mile (5 km) radius west of Thornton, near Bradford.

Powerful in mind and body

Victorian novelist Elizabeth Gaskell described Yorkshire people thus:

"They are a race powerful both in mind and body, both for good and for evil."

Sounds like a back-handed compliment to me.

Strange and queer
Charles Dickens said of Harrogate:

"The queerest place, with the strangest people in it, leading the oddest lives."

Well, it takes one to know one, they say.

Booze but no pub

Show me the way to Booze …
it's actually a place in Swaledale
from Old English words *boga* (bend in
a beck) and *hus* (house). In the 1400s
it was recorded as Bowehous. Today's
name is much more attractive but
sadly there's no pub.

A crackpot idea

Many a photograph has been taken
by a wife of her husband standing by
the signpost for Crackpot. It's a place
in Swaledale from the Old Norse
word *kraka* (meaning crow) and
Middle English *potte* (meaning
pothole).

Get straight to the point
The Stamford Bridge Pear Pie
commemorates a turning point in the
Battle of Stamford Bridge in 1066
when a soldier sailed under the
bridge in a malting tub and speared
a Viking guard.

Don't lose your head
It is said that the headless skeleton of
Thomas Cromwell was secretly
buried at Newburgh Priory, near
Coxwold, once the home of
Cromwell's daughter Mary
Fauconberg.

Noisy neighbours

The ghosts of marching Roman soldiers have been heard marching in the cellars of the Treasurer's House, one of York's oldest buildings and erected on the site of Roman barracks.

Cheersh...

Ulph's Horn is a two-foot (60 cm) drinking vessel made from an elephant's tusk, and one of York Minster's many treasures. It was given by Danish chief Ulph in the eleventh century when he handed over land to the Church.

Come blow your horn

For more than 700 years a horn had
been sounded nightly during autumn
and winter months, at Bainbridge in
Wensleydale, originally to guide
travellers through the local forests.
Now it just wakes the village's
sleeping children.

Petrified in Knaresborough

Knaresborough's Petrfying Well, or Dropping Well, where objects are 'petrified' through contact with elements in the water, is not a well at all. The water runs down and through a cliff. The Petrifying Well, along with Mother Shipton's Cave, is said to be the oldest registered visitor attraction in Britain, opening for the first time in 1630.

The luck of the silver thread
Folklore says that if you see a rare
'silver thread' (trapped air) in the
Ebbing and Flowing Well, situated at
the foot of Buckhaw Brow, near
Settle, good fortune will come your
way. However, bad luck may also
befall you, as the well's at the side of
a very busy road.

Getting hitched

The Hitching Stone, near the
Airedale village of Cowling, is
said to be the largest boulder in
Yorkshire at an estimated 1,200
tons. But this time it was supposed
to be Rombald's wife and not the
mythical giant himself who was
responsible for this bit of
moorland detritus.

Make a wish

One of the weirdly shaped Brimham Rocks is called the Wishing Stone. It has a hole into which you place the fingers of your right hand and then make a wish. If your fingers get stuck you'll wish you'd never bothered.

The Walking Parson

The Rev A N Cooper (born 1850)
was known as the Walking Parson.
He once walked from Filey to Rome
(741 miles/1,185 km) in six weeks.
He regularly tramped thirty miles
(48 km) a day.

Britain's only municipal railway
Bradford Corporation once ran the only municipally owned railway in the country. It was Nidd Valley Light Railway which carried passengers from 1907 to 1929.

...and Britain's oldest railway

Middleton Railway, two miles (3 km) from Leeds city centre, is reputedly to be the world's oldest railway. Permission to build it was made in 1758. Today it is run by rail enthusiasts.

Look to the skies

The largest recorded meteorite to bash into Britain landed near Wold Newton in the East Riding back in 1795. It is now back in alien lands — it's in the National History Museum in London.

Age-old problem of vandalism
Graffiti isn't a modern scourge —
Bronze Age types etched their
handiwork on stones on Ilkley Moor.
The symbol of fire, or the Sun, on
the Swastika Stone there was created
some 2,500 years ago.

A touch of glass

York Minster is the largest Gothic building in northern Europe, took 252 years to build and contains 128 stained-glass windows.

History and heritage a-plenty
Yorkshire is home to two UNESCO World Heritage sites, Studley Royal and Saltaire Village; it is also home to around fourteen per cent of England's ancient monuments (more than 2,600); and it has 800 conservation areas, and 116 registered parks and gardens.

Plenty of room for everyone
The Yorkshire Dales National Park
embraces 680 square miles
(1,755 km^2) of land but has a
resident human population of only
21,000 ... that's around twenty
acres (8 ha) per person. Thankfully,
sheep do most of the 'gardening'.

Lake land

Forget the Lake District —
Yorkshire has the honour of
containing England's highest lake:
Malham Tarn in the Dales sits
1,237 feet (377 m) above sea-level.

Jilted and jumping

In 1776 a young lady from Rigton, so upset at losing her man, flung herself off Almscliffe Crag. However, her skirts billowed out and she landed safely. Perhaps an early contender for the first parachute descent?

Standing tall

Standing around twenty feet (6 m) high, Duggleby Howe in the East Riding is the largest Neolithic barrow in the country; it could have been the site of a mass cremation.

A cross word

Lilla's Cross is said to be the oldest
cross on the North York Moors, and
marks the burial site of Lilla who was
killed when trying to save Edwin, a
seventh-century Christian king, from
an assassin.

Feast day

Wilfra Feast is the local name for the festival commemorating St Wilfrid's return from exile in AD 686 to his monastery in Ripon. It's held on the first Saturday before the first Monday in August.

Bring a bottle

On being appointed Archbishop of York in 1464, George Neville put on a mammoth 'spread' at Cawood which included 1,000 sheep, 2,000 pigs, 500 deer and 15,000 birds. Were indigestion tablets available in those days?

The world's largest church?

St Peter's Church in Warmsworth, near Doncaster, could be considered one of the largest churches in the world; its belfry is actually situated half a mile (800 m) from the the rest of the building.

Set in its ways
St John's Church at Goldthorpe, near
Doncaster, is thought to be the first
church made out of concrete.

Never-never land

The Yorkshire Motor Car Company in 1897 became the first British firm to sell vehicles to the public on the 'never-never' (hire purchase).

Slow coach

The first public stagecoach travelling from York to London in 1658 took four days — and no toilets or buffet car on board.

Neighbours from hell

Wakefield Zoo opened in 1839, but didn't last long after a bear escaped from its pen and mauled one of the zoo's neighbours in her garden.

A hefty heifer

The Craven Heifer is today known mainly for being a pub but in 1897 it really was a heifer — and a big 'un at that. It was over eleven feet (3.4 m) long, five feet two inches (1.6 m) tall at the shoulder and had a girth around its middle of ten feet two inches (3.1 m). The beast belonged to Rev William Carter of Bolton Abbey.

Move over Dick Whittington
William Craven, born in 1549 at a
small cottage in Appletreewick in the
Yorkshire Dales, sought fame and
fortune and went on to become Lord
Mayor of London.

The rich list

In the nineteenth century the top five land-owning individuals in Yorkshire were: Lord Londesborough (52,655 acres/21,309 ha); the Earl of Feversham (39,312/15,909); John Bowes of Streatlam Castle (34,887/14,118); Sir Tatton Sykes (34,010/13,763); the Earl of Harewood (29,078/11,767).

A heck of a name

By 'eck, Eckersecker is a heck of a name; it's a place in Dentdale and originally meant Hacker's Acre.

A clout round the rear
Only in Yorkshire will you find a
place named Rear Clouts. It means
'boundary rock-pile' from Old Norse
hreyrr and Old English *clud*, and can
be found on the boundary between
Craven and the Forest of
Knaresborough.

Pancake day

Pancake Rock near the Cow & Calf
on Ilkley Moor bears cup and ring
markings made by prehistoric
dwellers from around 4,000 years
ago. Wonder if they were baht 'at?

Anyone seen an arrow?

South of the River Ure at Boroughbridge stand three monoliths known as the Devil's Arrows. In the sixteenth century there were four; one disappeared probably to build a bridge … or maybe the Devil needed it back?

Cash and dash

Bradford for cash,
Halifax for dash,
Wakefield for pride and poverty;
Huddersfield for show,
Sheffield what's low,
Leeds for dirt and vulgarity.

That's how A R Wright summed up
the West Riding in the 1920s.

On the run from the law

At Penhill crags he tore his rags,
At Hunter's Thorn he blew his horn,
At Capplebank Stee [stile] he brak his knee,
At Griskill beck he brak his neck,
At Waddam's he couldn't fend,
At Griskill End will be his end.

Doggerel accompanying the tradition
of Burning of Bartle (a pig stealer) at
West Witton in Wensleydale.

Blazing besoms

Susannah Goor (1728-1826) had a reputation for fortune-telling and frightening small children. Folklore has it that she was associated with the Devil and was last seen when she "flew ower Driffield Church on a blazin' besom".

Philanthropy in action

In 1740 John Yorke of Bewerley Hall near Pateley Bridge forked out some of his hard-earned cash to keep locals occupied during times of economic hardship by getting them to build a folly at Guisecliff overlooking Nidderdale; Yorke's Folly is known locally as Two Stoups.

England's tallest cliff-face
At 660 feet (203 m), Boulby Cliff, between Staithes and Saltburn, is the tallest cliff-face in England.

A head of steam

The North Yorkshire Moors Railway
is the longest steam-operated railway
in the UK, with over eighteen miles
(29 km) of track.

Tunnel vision
Standedge Tunnel on the
Huddersfield Narrow Canal near
Marsden is the highest, longest and
deepest canal tunnel in the country,
at around 3 ¼ miles (5 km) long.

Starting small

In the Domesday Book of 1086, Leeds, now Yorkshire's biggest city, was described as a 'large farming village'.

An uncivil war

In 1642, Leeds was occupied by Royalists during the Civil War, but they were there for only a year as they were driven out by Lord Fairfax.

To 'croak it' is no joke

Sir Marmaduke Constable died in 1528 and is buried at St Oswald's, Flamborough. He fought at the battle of Flodden Field but it is said he 'croaked it' after swallowing a toad.

A memorable hymn

The words for *Onward Christian Soldiers* were written by Sabine Baring-Gould in 1865 for the annual children's Whitsun procession from St John's Church, at Horbury Bridge near Wakefield, to St Peter's in neighbouring Horbury.

Attendance record

An old tradition in the lonely hills around Swaledale was to include a sheepskin in the coffin of deceased shepherds.

This supposedly proved on Judgement Day that their irregular attendance at church could be forgiven.

Loose women
A gammerstong is a North Yorkshire term for an immoral or wanton woman … anyone got her phone number?

Hard labour

Did you know there was a patron saint of women in difficult labour? He's a Yorkshireman, St John of Bridlington, who was born at Thwing in 1319.

Food for thought
It is thought that the first recorded recipe for Yorkshire pudding was written in 1737 when it was called 'A Dripping Pudding'.

Cod almighty

A cod fish was caught near Scarborough in 1755 which measured five feet eight inches (1.72 m), had a girth of five feet (1.5 m) and weighed in at 76 lb (34.5 kg). The monster was sold for a shilling.

Whale meat again

More than 3,000 whales were landed by Whitby's whaling fleet during the eighteenth century.

Homes for all

When it was built in 1935, Quarry Hill Estate in Leeds was the largest council housing development in the country. It occupied twenty-eight acres (11 ha) of land and housed 3,000 people.

Britain's first twin town
Keighley was the first town in Britain to be 'twinned' with another from Europe. In 1905 Keighley organised a plan similar to twinning with Suresnes and Puteaux, and then on formal terms in 1920 with Poix-du-Nord, also in France.

York's first archbishop

St Paulinus was the first archbishop of York at the original minster and is credited with converting King Edwin to Christianity in the seventh century.

Say aaah
St Peter's in York was the first hospital in the country. It opened early in the tenth century thanks to the canons of York Minster.

Rabbiting on

A claim to fame for St Mary's Parish Church, built in 1120 AD in Beverley, is a carving of a rabbit, said to have inspired the White Rabbit in Lewis Carroll's *Alice's Adventures in Wonderland*.

Tree-mendous

The Cowthorpe Oak, situated near Wetherby, was once thought to be the oldest tree in Britain, a sapling during the Roman occupation; sadly, it is no longer alive.

Room with a view

Ingleborough Hill in the Yorkshire Dales provided the Celts with the ultimate 'room with a view'; here the locals built the loftiest hillfort in the country.

A round table

At a cave intriguingly called Navvy Noodle Hole, near Grassington in Wharfedale, the bones were found of twelve men sitting in a ring … 2,000 years after they had died.

Going with the flow
The River Swale is reputedly
England's fastest-flowing river.
Its name comes from the
Anglo-Saxon word *Sualuae*
meaning rapid and liable to deluge.

Mind the gap

Dog Laup, in Staithes, is the county's narrowest street at only twenty inches (51 cm) wide.

Yorkshire Prime Ministers

Three Yorkshiremen have become Prime Minister: Charles Wentworth of Rotherham (Prime Minister in 1765-6 and 1782); Herbert Henry Asquith of Morley (1908-16); and Harold Wilson of Cowlersley (1964-70 & 1974-6).

Rough justice
On 30th March 1694,
seventeen-year-old John
Collens was executed at
Micklegate Bar, York, for
stealing lead and copper from
Scarborough Church.

Ha, you missed!

Legend has it that the Devil, angered at the building of All Saints' Church on a pagan sacred hill at Rudston in the East Riding, hurled the Rudston Megalith at the building, but by divine intervention his aim was deflected and the stone landed in its present position. It is Britain's tallest standing stone, or megalith, at twenty-five feet (7.5 m) tall and weighing around forty tons.

Pig sick

It is said that if Whitby fishermen
see a pig on the way to their boats,
they believe it to be so unlucky
they won't put to sea.

Where did you get that hat?
The Staithes bonnet, traditionally
worn by the good women of that
parish, is of Viking influence. The
distinctive flap of the bonnet is to
prevent yucky stuff running down
their necks as they carry baskets of
fish or bait on their heads.

Make a wish

A candle shortage in Swaledale
during the seventeenth century
could be blamed on Henry
Jenkins. Then again, no birthday
cakes would have been big enough
to accommodate the number
needed for the Bolton-on-Swale
man who lived to be 169.
He died in 1670.

Danger and daring-do

In 1906, twenty-one-year-old Lily Cove was looking to become the first female parachutist and took to the skies over Haworth in a hot-air balloon. She leapt from a great height, but unfortunately became detached from her parachute and died. The Londoner is buried in Haworth cemetery.

Looking rough
Beware the Barton Bulldogs …
they're not actual dogs but
what locals call rough waves
on the River Humber.

A deadly wager

Dearbought Field, near Austwick in Three Peaks country, supposedly got its name after a farmer said that another chap could have the field if he could plough it in a day. The man managed the task by sundown but then dropped dead beside his plough.

Playing gooseberry

"My goosegogs are bigger than yours" is probably how the annual Egton Bridge Gooseberry Show started its annual competition to find the heaviest six gooseberries. The event is held on the first Tuesday in August.

Eerie drumbeats

Eerie drumming noises emanating from a well at Harpham in the East Riding are said to forecast the death of a member of the local St Quinton family — one of whose ancestors once knocked a drummer boy into the well.

A dispiriting journey

The A64 between York and Norton is said to be haunted by the spirit of Nance. She was due to marry a mail-coach driver but instead fell for a highwayman who later left her and their baby to die of exposure on the lonely road.

Ridings for ever

You are committing a cardinal sin if you state that the Ridings of Yorkshire no longer exist. They have been around for more than 1,100 years and were not replaced during the county boundary reorganisations in 1974.

Going for gold
In the London 2012 Olympics,
Yorkshire finished with seven gold
medals, two silver and three bronzes,
placing it twelfth in the medal table
if regarded as an independent
country … which, of course,
it should be.

Other books published by Dalesman:

The Little Book of Yorkshire
The Little Book of Yorkshire Humour
The Little Book of Yorkshire Dialect
The Little Book of Yorkshire Christmas
The Little Book of Dickie Bird
The Little Book of Lancashire
The Little Book of the Lake District
The Little Book of Country Sayings

For a full list of our books, calendars, DVDs, videos and magazines, visit www.dalesman.co.uk.